CONTENTS

INTRODUCTION

Yorkshire's history encompasses the past lives of monks in the monasteries, the sheep farmers high up on the Dales, affluent gentry in their Victorian houses, fisher-folk along the dramatic coastline, workers in the teeming new cities, and coal miners, working the rich seams of South Yorkshire to fuel the county's steel mills. The middle part of Yorkshire, the old West Riding, originally extended down to Sheffield, and was the powerhouse for the industrialisation of woollen and textile manufacturing. A ready supply of sheep in the upper dales, and an ingenuity in its people for inventing looms and spinning machines, meant that the West Riding was at the forefront of a global trade in textiles. Towns such as Leeds, Bradford, Halifax and Huddersfield grasped the opportunities to trade in wool, and developed along the fast-flowing rivers which originally gave power to their mills. Later, the combination of the factory system and the application of steam power created great wealth in the textile-producing towns and cities, which was then invested in splendid civic buildings in the area and eventually transformed the stinking slums of the Industrial Revolution into the vibrant towns and cities of today. The northern Dales contain the National Park; Victorian authors and artists came here to seek inspiration, but the area was also important for lead mining, smelt mills and stone quarrying. Along Yorkshire's coast are quaint villages and Victorian spas. Scarborough was the first town where the commercial possibilities of a seaside holiday were exploited, although in the early days it attracted the gentry for health reasons, rather than pleasure seekers from the urban West Riding. The whole coastline is dotted with villages clinging to the side of steep and constantly eroding cliffs, which attract visitors in search of picturesque views. King George III is said to have temporarily escaped from his mental madness after gazing at the vista from Ravenscar to Robin Hood's Bay.

ROBIN HOOD'S BAY, 1886 18195

YORKSHIRE DIALECT WORDS AND PHRASES

'Addling brass' – earning money.

'Agate' – to be busy or occupied with something.

'Appen' – perhaps.

'Baht' – without.

'Beck' – a stream.

'Clammed' or **'clemmed'** – very cold, frozen through, also used to mean hungry.

'Dollypawed' – left-handed.

'Dowly' – miserable damp or dreary weather.

'Featherlegged' – very tired.

'Fendable' – capable.

'Fettle' – to clean something, or to put it in good order.

'Fuzzock' – a donkey.

'Gennel', 'ginnel' or **'jennel'** – a narrow alleyway between houses.

'Mafting', as in **'It's mafting'** – the weather's really hot.

'It fair trim'd ma' – that suited me perfectly, as of a present.

'Keks' – trousers.

'Laikin' – skiving off school or work.

'Loiner' – an inhabitant of Leeds, derived from the word 'Loin' for a roll of cloth.

'Lop' – a flea.

'Mardy' – peevish, querulous, miserable, moody, sulking.

'Menseful' – neat, orderly. **'It will mense it off'** – It will finish it off nicely.

'Moudiwarp' – a mole.

'Mullock' – a mess or a muddle.

'Mytherin' – worrying about something, or being annoying – **'Stop mythering me!'**

'Nesh' – feeling the cold, as in **'I'm a bit nesh'.**

'Sackless' – lazy.

'Saig' – a saw, thus **'saigins'** meaning sawdust.

'Shoddy' – waste material from the mills, used to make low-grade cloth, blankets etc.

'Shuck' – crazy.

'Snicket' – a pathway, between hedges, fences etc.

'Spanish' – liquorice.

'Stagnated' or **'fair capp'd'** – greatly surprised.

'Taffled' – tangled.

'Throng' – busy.

'Worrawolly' – a simpleton, fool.

HAUNTED YORKSHIRE

In 1312 Piers Gaveston was ordered by Edward II to defend Scarborough Castle against rebel lords, but he was forced to surrender when food ran out and he was executed by the king's enemies. His headless spirit is said to haunt the castle ruins, trying to lure people over the edge of the walls to fall down the cliffs to their deaths. Some visitors have reported feeling a strange sensation, like a pushing hand, and the sound of laughter.

Be careful if you walk on Huddersfield's Castle Hill late at night – people have reported hearing sounds of fighting, and phantom horses galloping to some ghostly battlefield.

A ghost story from York concerns the Treasurer's House, where a young apprentice plumber working in the cellar heard a trumpet playing, then saw Roman soldiers marching by, but as if on their knees. When the cellar floor was dug up, evidence of a Roman road was discovered where the soldiers' feet would have been.

During the Civil War, Bradford was besieged by the Royalist forces of the Earl of Newcastle. He was so enraged by the resistance of the people of Bradford that one night he went to bed declaring that when the town was taken, he would slaughter every man, woman and child in the place. He was woken by a ghost standing beside him, wringing its hands and moaning 'Pity poor Bradford!'. The earl was so shaken that he changed his plan, and decided to only attack those who resisted him.

An old folklore belief in the Leeds area was that the souls of babies who died before they were baptised would return to haunt their parents, in the shape of devil dogs known as Gabble Retchets.

When Bram Stoker, author of 'Dracula', stayed in Whitby he noted 'there is a legend that a white lady is seen in one of the windows' of the ruins of Whitby Abbey. The 'ghost', known as 'Lady Hilda', was believed to be that of St Hilda, founder of the abbey, and appeared as a shrouded figure in the highest window of the north side of the ruins; it was probably an illusion caused by the sun shining on the window at a certain time and angle.

The ghost of Mary, Queen of Scots, is said to haunt the Turret House of Sheffield Manor Lodge (see photograph S108703, page 21), where she spent part of her long period of captivity in the reign of Elizabeth I. There have been several reported sightings of a beautiful lady dressed in black who glides across the floor and disappears through walls, and a ghostly face is said to sometimes look out from a window of the Turret House.

HULL, ST ANDREW'S DOCK c1955 HI33037

YORKSHIRE MISCELLANY

One of the county's most important prehistoric monuments is The Devil's Arrows, near the A1 near Boroughbridge in north Yorkshire. The stones are taller than most of the Stonehenge megaliths and stand in a line running north to south, apparently aligned on the most southerly Midsummer rising moon. A folklore belief was that you could raise the Devil if you walked anti-clockwise around the stones twelve times at midnight.

Scarborough Castle dates back to 1160, but there is evidence that Bronze Age and Iron Age people lived on the promontory here, and the remains of a Roman signal post are still visible within the walls of the castle. In 1980 a Bronze Age sword was found there which is about 3,000 years old; it was found almost perfectly preserved, not broken, and can be seen at the visitor centre at the castle.

Ilkley's famous Saxon crosses are shown in the graveyard of All Saints' Church in photograph 7290 (opposite). The central pillar dates from AD850, while the cross added in 1884 had been made from two separate stones. Carvings on this pillar depict the four evangelists, St Matthew, Mark, Luke and John. The crosses are thought to have been burial monuments. They were removed from the graveyard in 1983 and are now preserved inside the church tower.

It was the Viking Danes who settled in Yorkshire who first divided the county into the 'ridings', three historic subdivisions of the county (North, East and West Riding) which were abolished in 1974 under local government reorganisation. Originally, they were called 'thridings', or thirds. That ancient Norse heritage is still evident today in many Yorkshire place-names, especially in place-names ending in '-by', '-ness' and '-thorpe'.

**ILKLEY, ALL SAINTS' CHURCH,
THE SAXON CROSSES IN THE CHURCHYARD c1874** 7290

In Roman times the city of York was the principal military base in Britain, and it was at York in AD306 that Constantine the Great was proclaimed emperor by his army – he went on to make Christianity the official religion of the Roman Empire. A modern statue of Constantine stands outside York Minster, but a marble head of him sculpted in Roman times, found in Stonegate, can be seen in the Yorkshire Museum in the city.

York Minster is famous for wonderful Gothic architecture, woodwork and stonework, and especially stained glass, 128 windows in all. It is particularly famous for its magnificent Rose Window and the beautiful west window with heart-shaped tracery, known as 'the Heart of Yorkshire'. The wonderful stained glass window above the high altar was made in the 13th century and is larger than a tennis court. Re-leading of the window was begun when it was removed from the minster for safety during the Second World War; the mammoth task took ten years to complete.

In the 9th century the Vikings took over York, calling it 'Jorvik'. The last Viking king of Jorvik was the delightfully-named Eric Bloodaxe, who died in AD954. Excavations have turned up many artefacts from this period, which can be seen at The Jorvik Viking Centre. Even the Viking rubbish dumps were a treasure trove to the archaeologists: shoes, utensils and items of discarded clothing all serve to illuminate the Viking way of life.

Street names in York can be confusing: the historic gateways into York are called 'bars'; the term 'gate' (ie Stonegate, Walmgate) actually means 'street' and derives from the old Viking word 'gata'; a 'yard' is an alley, and a 'court' is a yard.

A 16th-century York woman, Margaret Clitheroe, was canonised by Pope Paul VI in 1970 as St Margaret of York. Margaret was married to a butcher and lived in the Shambles. She was arrested for harbouring Roman Catholic priests, and sentenced to death in 1586 by the barbaric method of 'pressing', or being crushed to death beneath a board. A house in the Shambles is now set aside as a shrine to her.

Many notorious criminals were tried at York Assize Court, including the highwayman Dick Turpin in 1739. He spent his final days in the condemned cell of York's prison, and was hanged at the gallows at Tyburn, on the Tadcaster Road. Dick Turpin's grave can be seen in St George's churchyard. Turpin is famous in folklore for a legendary ride on his famous horse, Black Bess, from London to York, but this ride was actually done 60 years earlier by another highwayman, William Nevison, who was also hanged at York, in 1684.

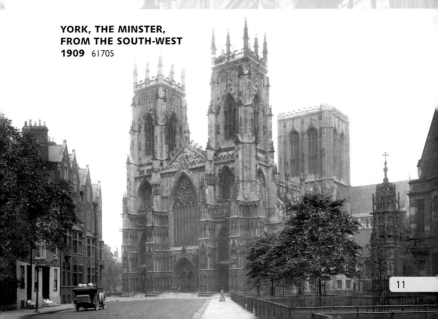

YORK, THE MINSTER, FROM THE SOUTH-WEST 1909 61705

Did You Know?
YORKSHIRE
A MISCELLANY

YORK, THE SHAMBLES 1909 61722

The medieval chapel on the bridge at Wakefield shown in photograph W464002 (below) is the only surviving chantry chapel in the town. The building was renovated in 1848, but within forty years smoke and pollution had again damaged the pinnacles. The old chapel front was purchased during renovation and can still be found sited by the lake at Kettlethorpe Hall.

The battle of Wakefield in 1460, at which Richard, Duke of York was killed, was one of the major battles of the Wars of the Roses.

WAKEFIELD, THE CHANTRY c1953 W464002

RIPON, THE CATHEDRAL c1955 R38012

The minster at Ripon became a cathedral in 1836. The author Lewis Carroll (real name Charles Lutwidge Dodgson) was the son of the first Canon of Ripon Cathedral, and visited his father here regularly over many years. He first told his tale of Alice in Wonderland in July 1862, after ten years of visits to Ripon and its cathedral, and was probably inspired by the cathedral carvings, including the curious creatures carved on the misericords (small wooden seats) in the choir. In photograph 67323 (below) we see a griffin chasing two rabbits – one of them is disappearing down a rabbit hole, just like the White Rabbit that Alice follows into Wonderland.

RIPON, CATHEDRAL, THE GRIFFIN AND RABBITS MISERICORD 1914
67323

FOUNTAINS ABBEY, SOUTH WEST 1895 35279

In 1132 a group of monks from St Mary's Abbey in York settled in the valley of the River Skell to found Fountains Abbey, which eventually became very wealthy thanks to the wool trade; the monks owned vast estates where they reared sheep. Henry VIII dissolved Fountains Abbey in 1540. The glorious Cistercian abbey remains remarkably well preserved, a delightful medley of lichen-covered ruins dating from the 12th to the 15th centuries which preserve the plan of this great monastery almost intact.

The town of Richmond owes its origins to its spectacularly defensive site high above the River Swale. Count Alan Rufus of Brittany, kinsman of William the Conqueror, built the castle c1071 as the headquarters of an immense area of feudal land-holdings later known as the Honour of Richmond. Most early Norman castles were motte and bailey earthworks, but Richmond was one of the first stone-built castles in the country. The magnificent keep was added by Conan, Duke of Brittany in the second half of the 12th century and is a magnificent example of Norman military architecture.

RICHMOND, THE CASTLE FROM THE GREEN 1898 41642

BEVERLEY, MARKET PLACE 1886 17885

Beverley began as a religious centre that developed from the monastery founded in the eighth century by John, Bishop of York, later canonised as St John of Beverley. The minster at Beverley is one of Europe's most beautiful and finest churches. In the Middle Ages the town also became an important centre of the textile industry, known for the production of high-quality cloth. During the Georgian period the town acquired the elegant houses and fine public buildings which gave it such a distinctive character and ensures its place among the forty English towns of the greatest historical interest.

Dominican friars (the 'Black Friars') arrived in Beverley in 1240 and as popular preachers attracted a strong following, with Beverlonians leaving bequests to the Friary rather than to one of the existing churches. The resulting antagonism of the minster clergy to the friars is given visual proof in a carving on one of the minster's misericords (small wooden seats), showing a fox in a friar's habit preaching to geese, representing those residents of Beverley foolish enough to listen.

Sheffield's cutlery industry was first recorded in 1297, when Robertus le coteler – Robert the cutler – was listed as a taxpayer. In 1624, 498 master craftsmen in Sheffield and the surrounding villages were recorded: 440 knife makers, 31 shear and sickle makers, and 27 scissor makers. By the mid 17th century the industry was run by master craftsmen – 'little mesters' – doing business from small workshops attached to their cottages or at water-powered grinding wheels. Here might be a coal-fuelled smithy where blades were forged, or small rooms where the handles were fitted or 'hafted', and where knives were finally assembled after the blades had been taken to a riverside cutlers' wheel to be ground on a grindstone. Sheffield's once-great cutlery industry has now all but disappeared. Viner's, once the largest cutlery firm in the country, went out of business in 1982; its name and trademark were sold, and now appear on imported Korean cutlery.

Sheffield's cathedral is famed for its Shrewsbury Chapel; among the monuments is one to the 6th Earl of Shrewsbury, who was burdened for many years with looking after Mary, Queen of Scots during her long period of captivity in England, from 1570 until 1584 (see photograph S108701, below). The Scottish queen was held captive in the castle at Sheffield, but from time to time she was moved from the castle to Sheffield Manor Lodge (photograph S108703, right). Elizabeth I's ministers were concerned that she might escape from this less fortified residence, but the earl's son assured them that 'unless she could transform herself into a flea or a mouse' it would be impossible for her to do so.

SHEFFIELD, THE TOMB OF GEORGE TALBOT IN THE CATHEDRAL 2005
S108701

SHEFFIELD, THE TURRET HOUSE,
SHEFFIELD MANOR LODGE 2005
S108703

The five rise locks at Bingley are part of the Leeds & Liverpool Canal, and are one of the wonders of the waterway system. They are known as staircase locks, because the top gate of each chamber is also the bottom one of the next: there is no water between the two.

BINGLEY, LOCKS ON THE LEEDS AND LIVERPOOL CANAL c1900 B98501

J. R. THORNTON

REGISTERED
709
LEEDS

Robert

The Town Hall at Leeds (photograph 34765, below) with its magnificent many-pillared clock tower was designed by the Hull architect Cuthbert Broderick, who also designed the Corn Exchange, and has been described as one of the best examples of the Classical revival style in England. Built between 1853 and 1858, this sumptuous public building was deliberately ambitious in scale, its dignified and spectacular classical lines symbolising the reputation of Leeds as the leading city of the West Ridings.

LEEDS, THE TOWN HALL 1894 34765

Thousands of people came to work in the textile towns and cities of the West Riding in the 19th century, but their living conditions were often appalling, with families crowded into a single room or cellars, and non-existent sanitation. Public health measures for the new industrial cities were not taken until several outbreaks of cholera resulted in thousands of deaths – cholera epidemics in Leeds alone killed 700 people in 1832 and over 2,000 in 1848-49. The factory chimneys continually churned out black, sulphurous smoke, and Bradford gained the reputation of being the most polluted town in England.

One of the few 19th-century mill owners concerned about the smoke produced by the industrial mills and factories was Titus Salt, who eventually became the largest employer in Bradford. He discovered that Rodda Smoke Burners produced very little pollution, and in 1842 he had these placed in all his premises. He became mayor of Bradford in 1848, but his failure to persuade the council to pass a bylaw making Rodda Smoke Burners compulsory in all the local mills and factories was one of the factors that prompted him to build his state-of-the-art textile mill and model industrial village of Saltaire, three miles outside Bradford. His mill there was the largest in Europe – the weaving shed housed 1,200 looms and a workforce in excess of 3,000.

The foundation stone for the Wool Exchange in Bradford was laid by Lord Palmerston in 1864. This proud trade house in the Venetian Gothic style was home to 3,000 dealers, with buyers and sellers trading wool from West Yorkshire, the Colonies and the Far East. It was said that whatever the type of wool or hair, a buyer would be found at the Bradford Exchange, and that when traders were about their buying and selling on Mondays and Thursdays, the place had the atmosphere of a madhouse. The Wool Exchange has now been sympathetically restored, and the ground floor is used by Waterstone's bookshop.

BRADFORD, FORSTER SQUARE
1897 39506x

Photograph 39506x (opposite) shows the statue of Richard Oastler, 'the Factory King', in its original position in Forster Square in Bradford; the statue was later moved to Rawson Square, and in recent years was moved again to its present site on North Parade. Richard Oastler fought against the use of child labour in the industrial mills. Yorkshire mill owners were at the forefront when it came to employing child labour in the 18th and 19th centuries. In the early days of the industrial revolution, those who ended up in the mills around Leeds were luckier than the children sent to Bradford: in Leeds they only had to work a 12-hour day, against a 13-hour day in Bradford, and even children as young as five were sometimes expected to work these long hours.

In the 19th century all workers who handled wool, animal hair and hides risked catching anthrax. These products were such an important part of Bradford's trade and industry, and the deadly disease so prevalent amongst its workers, that anthrax at one time was known as the Bradford Disease. In the 1890s Frederick William Eurich was appointed to work in a laboratory in Bradford. After years of experiments which put himself in considerable danger, Eurich realised that the disease was transferred to humans when they came into contact with blood from an infected animal. The use of formaldehyde, rigorous precautions and inspection of wool and other fibres led to a decrease in cases of anthrax, and in later years the development of antibiotics provided a cure for the disease. Eurich was awarded the Gold Medal of the Textile Institute in recognition of the thousands of lives in the textile industry that were saved as a result of his work.

MILL WORKERS F6039

HALIFAX, TOWN HALL 1900 H9001

Set in the foothills of the Pennines, Halifax is one of the great cloth towns of England and has been a producer of cloth since the 13th century. At its height in the 19th and early 20th century, Halifax was the greatest of the textile towns of West Yorkshire, a centre for woollen manufacture and clothing, larger even than Leeds or Bradford. The Town Hall, in the background of photograph H9001 (above), was designed in the Italian style by Sir Charles Barry in 1863, and is famous for its extraordinary-looking clock tower.

The cloth industry was so important to Halifax that in medieval times the town was granted its own laws for dealing with people convicted of stealing cloth; those found guilty were beheaded on a guillotine-like contraption called the 'Halifax Gibbet'. The Halifax Gibbet Law was limited to the forest of Hardwick and the 18 towns and villages within its boundary. Anyone found with stolen cloth 'shall be taken to the gibbet and there have his head cut from his body'. This law, combined with the harsh anti-vagrancy laws of Hull, gave rise to the saying 'From Hull, Hell and Halifax, good Lord deliver us.'

Harewood House, between Leeds and Harrogate, is one of Yorkshire's finest stately homes. It was designed by John Carr and Robert Adam, and the 1,000 acre parkland was created by 'Capability' Brown. The north front of the house was remodelled in 1843 by the great Victorian architect Sir Charles Barry, who also designed the Houses of Parliament. The house contains many treasures, including an unrivalled collection of 18th-century furniture made especially for Harewood by the great furniture designer Thomas Chippendale, who was born at Otley in West Yorkshire.

HAREWOOD, HAREWOOD HOUSE c1886 7365

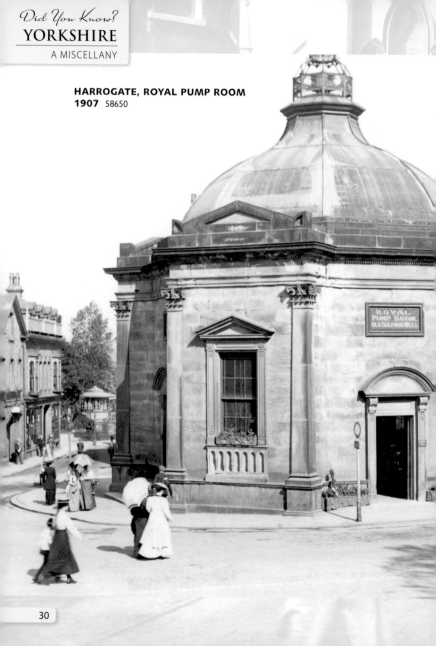

**HARROGATE, ROYAL PUMP ROOM
1907** 58650

ROYAL
PUMP ROOM
OLD SULPHUR WELL

Harrogate claims to have the world's strongest known sulphur springs, the result of magmatic or plutonic waters rising from deep within the earth's crust. The sulphurous water which made the place famous as a spa town was a recommended cure for the intestinal worms and other kinds of internal parasites which in the late 17th century were said to have affected much of the population. One of the strangest things about Harrogate's famous mineral wells is that, of the scores of springs which reach the surface, no two are exactly alike in the chemical analysis of their water.

The only hostile incident which directly affected Harrogate during the Second World War was the dropping of three bombs on the Hotel Majestic in September 1940 – none of the bombs exploded, however. One of the unexploded bombs was found standing upright in an upstairs room by soldiers sent to investigate. The men mistook it for a water tank, and used the hotel lift to take it out. After the bomb had been safely defused, the casing was used to raise money for the Harrogate Spitfire Fund. Captured German documents revealed that the Germans had believed that the hotel was being used by the Air Ministry, but a newspaper claimed at the time that the pilot had once been refused a table at the Majestic's restaurant before the war, and had bombed the hotel in revenge for the snub.

The theme music of the long-running BBC radio programme 'The Archers' was composed by Arthur Wood, a former choirboy at St Peter's Church in Harrogate and deputy conductor of the Harrogate Municipal Orchestra. Mr Wood wrote the music as the Barwick Green movement in his symphony entitled 'My Native Heath'.

The River Nidd which flows through Harrogate and Knaresborough has an ancient Celtic name which is thought to mean 'brilliant water', what we might today call 'sparkling'.

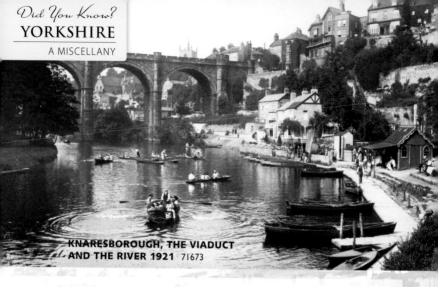

KNARESBOROUGH, THE VIADUCT AND THE RIVER 1921 71673

One of the great characters of 18th-century Yorkshire was Jack Metcalf, ('Blind Jack of Knaresborough'), the road-maker responsible for many turnpike roads constructed in the district, including the Boroughbridge turnpike and the road between Harrogate and Harewood Bridge – his accurate measuring device, the Viameter Wheel, can be seen in the Castle Museum at Knaresborough. Jack was born in Knaresborough in 1717 and was blinded by smallpox at the age of six. He served as an engineer and bandsman under General Wade in Scotland, where he learnt the skills of road-building. A man of many talents, he was invited to Harrogate to become the resident fiddler at the Queen's Head Hotel in 1732 and became a popular local celebrity. He later scandalously eloped with the daughter of the Granby Hotel's landlord on the eve of her wedding.

During the reign of King John (1199-1216) the castle at Knaresborough served as a royal arsenal for the manufacture of 'quarrels', the missiles fired from crossbows – these missiles had a four-sided sharply pointed metal head, which could cause considerable damage to buildings and fearsome wounds. The phrase 'to pick a quarrel' derives from the crossbow-man choosing the best weapon to use against a particular target.

Doncaster owes its transformation from an agricultural to an industrial centre to the coming of the railways. The Great Northern Railway chose Doncaster for the site of its locomotive and carriage and wagon workshops. Coal mining was also a major employer, and the town was ringed with pit villages. The first sod was cut at Brodsworth Colliery in 1905 and at Hatfield Main in 1911. At Hatfield it took five years to reach the Barnsley bed, at 852 yards below the surface.

The Crusaders of the 12th century probably introduced the liquorice plant to Pontefract, and from that grew a hugely important industry; it still flourishes today, but the liquorice roots are no longer grown locally. The disc-shaped sweets flavoured with liquorice known as Pontefract Cakes (or 'Pomfret' or 'Pomfrey' Cakes) are still made in the town, and an annual liquorice festival is held there, where liquorice flavoured cheese, ice cream and beer can be sampled. Liquorice is known as 'Spanish' in some parts of Yorkshire.

DONCASTER, STATION ROAD 1903 49854

HUDDERSFIELD, ASPLEY BASIN 2005 H151702

The growth of Huddersfield into one of the most important textile towns in Britain can be traced back to 1671, when John Ramsden obtained a market charter from Charles II. Huddersfield was at the junction of two river valleys, had good access to Leeds, Bradford and Halifax, and was on the trans-Pennine routes. By the mid 18th century local clothiers were part of an international trade that linked them with markets all over Britain and overseas. The Ramsdens tapped into this expanding trade, building Cloth Hall in 1766 and later opening the Ramsden Canal which connected Huddersfield, via the Calder Navigation, to Goole and Hull. In effect, Huddersfield became a port and the hub of the woollen industry. By the end of the 20th century the town's textile industry was in decline against foreign competition and economic forces. Mills closed, thousands of jobs were lost and the physical appearance of the town was transformed as familiar mills and their landmark chimneys disappeared. Although vestiges of the textile and other industries remain, the way of life and the rich culture they sustained are gone forever. Working in the mills was often a hard life, but there is no doubt that it engendered a strong sense of community, and that people felt great pride in their work.

Semer Water, the largest natural lake in Yorkshire, is about half a mile in length and covers about 100 acres (see photograph 82610 (below). It was formed by Ice Age glaciers forming in the side dale known as Raydale, and is drained by England's shortest river, the Bain, which runs into Wensleydale at Bainbridge.

The village of West Witton in Wensleydale holds an annual event known as the Bartle Burning, in which an effigy named Owd Bartle is carried around the village in a procession before being burnt. This custom takes place on the Saturday nearest to 24th August, the Feast Day of St Bartholomew, to whom the village church is dedicated, but its origins probably go back to pre-Christian times and may relate to a fertility god ritual.

SEMER WATER 1929 82610

Haworth, a small town set amidst the moors near Keighley, is a place of literary pilgrimage, for in the parsonage here lived the Brontë sisters, Emily, Charlotte and Anne, and their brother Branwell – their father was the vicar of St Michael and All Angels' Church. The moors around Haworth gave the sisters the inspiration for their novels, the most famous of which are 'Jane Eyre', 'Wuthering Heights' and 'The Tenant of Wildfell Hall'. A footpath leads out of Haworth up the moor to Top Withens, now a ruin, which is said to be the original of Heathcliff's farmstead in Emily Brontë's 'Wuthering Heights' (see photograph H194045, below).

The Tan Hill Inn, occupying a desolate moorland location on Sleightholme Moor between Swaledale and the valley of the Greta to the north, is the highest inn in England. For many years it was the site of an annual sheep sale; today it is a welcome refreshment stop for walkers on the Pennine Way. The inn is said to be haunted by the ghost of a former landlady, Mrs Peacock.

HAWORTH, TOP WITHENS, 'WUTHERING HEIGHTS' 1958 H194045

ASKRIGG, THE VILLAGE 1906 56021

The busy little town of Thirsk, between York and Darlington, is the heart of 'James Herriot Country'; the actual vet in the famous series of books about the life of a Yorkshire vet, real name Alf Wight, was married in St Mary's Church in Thirsk in 1941. The James Herriot books were made into the hugely popular BBC television series 'All Creatures Great and Small' in the 1970s and 1980s, using the village of Askrigg as a location.

Bainbridge was once the 'capital' of Upper Wensleydale. An ancient custom is still carried out here: every evening, from the Feast of the Holy Rood (27th September) to Shrove Tuesday in spring, a huge horn, which hangs in the Rose and Crown Hotel, is brought outside, and three long notes are blown. This tradition dates from Norman times, when Wensleydale was covered in dense forests, and Bainbridge was a safe haven for the foresters (and for travellers and drovers too). Every evening the horn blower would sound the horn to guide them all down from the lonely fells at dusk.

ILKLEY, THE GROVE 1911 63556

Ilkley found fame in the 19th century as a spa town after four Leeds businessmen chose a site in nearby Wheatley for their Ben Rhydding Hydro; when it opened for business in 1844 it was the very first purpose-built hydrotherapy centre in England. Hotels and other hydropathic establishments sprang up in the area, and soon Ilkley was 'the Malvern of the North'. The magnificent Ben Rhydding Hydro which had put Ilkley on the map was demolished in 1955, and houses were built on part of the site; it is remembered now in the name Hydro Close.

'On Ilkla Moor Baht'at' ('On Ilkley Moor Without a Hat') – so where did that song come from? The tune is from the hymn 'Cranbrook'. It is reputed that in 1886 a church choir from Halifax was holding its summer picnic high up on the moors near Ilkley. One of the young girls, called Mary Jane, wandered off with her sweetheart. When the couple returned, the rest of the choir teased them by bursting into song with new words to the tune: 'Where's tha bin since Ah saw thee? Tha's been a-courting Mary Jane'.

HULL, WHITEFRIARGATE 1903 49817

In April 1642, Charles I was refused entry to the city at the Beverley Gate, at the west end of Whitefriargate; this was the first action of defiance against the king, and set in motion the chain of events that resulted in the Civil War which eventually led to the king's death. It was in a room now known as the 'Plotting Parlour' in Ye Olde White Harte Inn (then the Governor's home) that the Governor and other leading citizens decided to follow Parliament's instructions and refuse to let Charles I enter Hull and take control of the arsenal that was stored in the city.

In 1759 William Wilberforce was born in Hull; his birthplace now holds an extensive collection of artefacts relating to the slave trade, the abolition of which was to take up most of his political life. William Wilberforce was elected MP for Hull at the age of 21. He was involved in many causes for reform, but is best remembered for his long campaign against slavery which resulted in the passing of a parliamentary bill to end the slave trade in 1807, and slavery being abolished in the British Empire in 1833 (this became law in 1834). Wilberforce died in 1833, and was buried in Westminster Abbey. He was named the Greatest Ever Yorkshireman in a BBC poll in 2000, and in June 2005 Archbishop Desmond Tutu praised him, saying that 'Wilberforce showed that each and every one of us can make a difference'.

Photograph S176001 (below) shows fish wives and old men at the attractive village of Staithes c1900, baiting the lines. The women are wearing traditional 'Staithes bonnets', which were flared at the sides to stop the coils of hooks and lines becoming entangled in their hair. Each bonnet required a yard of material, and was double-plaited at the front and tied at the back with a bow.

Tradition says that Scarborough was established in the 10th century by a Norseman nicknamed 'Skarthi' ('hare-lip') – the name of the settlement was originally 'Skathi's burg' ('Skarthi's stronghold'). Scarborough became a spa town after the therapeutic qualities of its water was discovered in the 1620s. The mineral waters of Scarborough contain a high content of magnesium sulphate, which means that the healing properties of the water are certainly as effective as Andrews Liver Salts.

STAITHES, BAITING THE LINES c1900 S176001

SCARBOROUGH, SOUTH BAY c1873 6560

Bathing machines are seen lined up on the beach at Scarborough in photograph 6560 (above), overlooked by the 365-bed Grand Hotel, which has 365 bedrooms, 52 chimneys, 12 floors and 4 turrets, representing the days, weeks, months and seasons of the year. Scarborough may have been the first resort on the north-east coast to introduce bathing machines on to its beach – there is a written record of them being hired out by three ladies in 1797.

On 17 August 1914, during the First World War, two German cruisers took up station off Scarborough and fired over 500 shells into the town. A number of people were killed, and this action spawned a slogan for the enlistment posters all over the country that urged young men to join up and fight the enemy. It ran: 'Remember Scarborough? Enlist Now!'

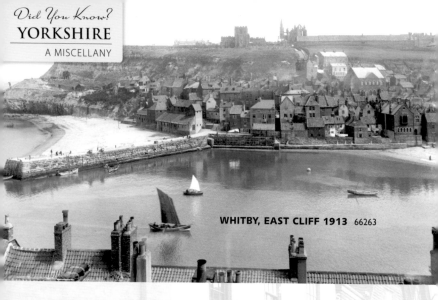

WHITBY, EAST CLIFF 1913 66263

St Mary's Church in Whitby was made famous by Bram Stoker in his Gothic novel 'Dracula' as the place where the count sought refuge in the grave of a suicide. The author stayed in Whitby, at Number 6, Royal Crescent, in 1890; it was here that he started to write his most famous book, setting much of it in the town.

Whaling was once a major part of Whitby's economy. Whale oil was very important in the past, used for lamp oil, lubrication, and for manufacturing soap, textiles, varnish, paint and explosives. One of Whitby's famous landmarks is the arch on West Cliff made from a pair of whale jaw bones. During the whaling years it was the custom to trice up a pair of whale jaw bones to the mast, decorated with ribbons, when a ship was returning to Whitby's harbour from a whaling trip, as a sign that the voyage had been successful.

In the 19th century Whitby was famous for jewellery and other items which local craftmen made from jet, a hard, black material which is actually fossilised wood from Araucaria trees (a type of Monkey Puzzle tree). Twenty million or so years ago there must have been a forest of these trees around the area, for Whitby's is one of the best deposits of jet anywhere in the world.

Captain James Cook, the famous navigator, surveyor and sea captain, was born in the Yorkshire village of Marton, near Middlesbrough, in 1728. He moved to Whitby at the age of seventeen, and was apprenticed to John and Henry Walker, local ship-owners – the Walkers' house in Grape Lane in Whitby is now the Captain Cook Memorial Museum. His first experience as a sailor was in 1747 when he embarked from Whitby on a coal carrier. He later joined the Navy, where he rose through the ranks, becoming master in 1759. He displayed exceptional ability as a navigator and surveyor, and in 1768, after surveying the St Lawrence River in Canada and the Newfoundland coast, he commanded the 'Endeavour' for the Royal Society expedition to the Pacific, Australia and New Zealand. This was the first of his three major expeditions, in each of which he sailed in ships built in Whitby. A statue of Captain Cook overlooks Whitby harbour from West Cliff. Cook has a map in one hand and dividers in the other and looks out to sea, his eyes on the distant horizon.

WHITBY, CAPTAIN COOK'S MONUMENT 1913 66270

SPORTING YORKSHIRE

There have been horseracing meetings in Doncaster since 1600, but it was the St Leger that put the town on the racing calendar. It was established by Lt Gen Anthony St Leger in 1776 and is the oldest classic race. Some race meetings at York were timed to coincide with York assizes, and the Knavesmire was the location for both horse racing and public executions from 1731. The introduction of two major races in the 1840s, the Ebor Handicap, and the Gimcrack Stakes, was the basis for the course's later success.

The Scarborough Amateur Rowing Club, founded in 1869, is the oldest surviving rowing club on the north-east coast. For more than 100 years sea rowing has taken place on the Yorkshire coast between the Tees and the Humber, sometimes known as the German Ocean Race, after the former name for the North Sea; the tradition began with friendly rivalry between the fisherman and the jet miners from Blyth.

The home of Yorkshire County Cricket Club is at Headingley, Leeds. County matches transferred to the ground in 1891 from the previous county pitch at Sheffield. Test cricket came in 1899, and rugby was first played here in 1895 by Leeds FC, one of the 20 original clubs that formed the Rugby League. The Headingley stadium is unique, as it is effectively two grounds, for both cricket and rugby, unified by a stand which has one side facing the cricket pitch and one side facing the rugby pitch.

In 1988 Scarborough FC sold naming rights for its stadium to McCain, the food manufacturer – the first time naming rights had been sold in this way in England.

The legendary Bill Shankley became manager of Huddersfield Town FC in 1956. One of his signings for the club was 15 year-old Denis Law, who went on to find fame as a Scottish international and Manchester United star. When Law was sold to Manchester City four years later for what was then a new British record transfer fee of £55,000, some of the money was used to finance the new floodlights at the Leeds Road ground. They became known as the 'Denis Law Lights'.

Sheffield is the home of the world's two oldest football clubs. Sheffield FC, founded in 1857, is still in existence, playing at the Don Valley Stadium. Hallam FC, founded three years later, is also still in existence, playing at its original ground, Sandygate. Bramall Lane, home of Sheffield United FC, is thought to be the oldest major ground which still hosts professional football matches. It is also one of only two grounds to have staged an England cricket match against Australia, an England football international, and an FA Cup final (the Oval in London is the other). The name of Sheffield Wednesday FC was originally 'the Wednesday Cricket Club'. A cricket team of that name was established in the early 19th century and later a football team was set up in association with it. For many years the football club was known as 'The Wednesday', before its official name was changed to Sheffield Wednesday FC in the late 1920s.

SALTAIRE, THE MILL AND THE CRICKET PITCH 1888 21024

For many decades Albert Geldard held the record as the youngest player ever to play League football. He was 15 years and 158 days old when he made his debut for Bradford (Park Avenue) FC in 1929. He also represented England before his 20th birthday. His record was broken in the 2008/09 season, when Reuben Noble-Lazarus came on to play for Barnsley Football Club at Ipswich Town aged 15 years and 45 days.

Bradford City AFC had an eventful and unique early history. Originally Manningham Rugby League Club, in 1903 the club switched to association football, and without having played a game was invited to join the Football League. This was an attempt to introduce soccer into a rugby-dominated area, and City was the first West Riding club in the League. Bradford City's unusual colours of claret and amber are distinctive; in opinion polls the shirt has been voted both best and worst shirt. City scarves are popular with fans of 'Harry Potter' books, as they are also the colours of Hogwarts School – and Bradford City actually had a player called Harry Potter before the First World War!

The famous and successful Leeds United Football Club of the late 1960s and early 1970s was notable for the continuity in its playing staff. Six players from this era made over 700 appearances for the club – Jack Charlton and Billy Bremner both played on 773 occasions – and three more players made more than 500 appearances.

Rugby League was founded at a meeting at the George Hotel in Huddersfield in 1895, when twenty-two clubs met at the George Hotel and formed the NRFU (Northern Rugby Football Union) as a breakaway group from the RFU (Rugby Football Union). This revolution in the world of rugby was sparked by the RFU's decision to enforce the amateur principle of the sport. The NRFU became the Rugby Football League in 1922.

Hull FC (Rugby League) holds two records in the game. Hull FC's Lee Jackson holds the record for the fastest ever try in a professional game; playing against Sheffield Eagles at the Don Valley Stadium in 1992, he scored after just nine seconds. In the 1978/79 season in Division Two, Hull FC won every game – the only time this has been achieved in professional Rugby League.

Since its formation as a 'super club' in 1963, City of Leeds Swimming Club has enjoyed great success in producing international medal winners. These have included Adrian Moorhouse, who won Olympic gold, Andy Astbury, who won Olympic bronze, and two World Championship winners, James Hickman and Claire Huddart. The club has won the National Club Championship on many occasions.

The swimming baths that used to stand in Ramsden Street in Huddersfield were where the 1960 Olympic champion Anita Lonsbrough trained. Born in Huddersfield in 1941, she worked at the Town Hall as a clerk. At the age of 19 she won a gold medal in the 200m breaststroke event at the 1960 Olympics in Rome in a thrilling final in world record time, and received a hero's welcome on her return home to Huddersfield. At one time in her career she held not only the Olympic gold medal but also the Empire and European gold medals at the same time. She also made sporting history by becoming the first woman to win the BBC Sports Personality of the Year award in 1962, and was the first woman to carry the flag for the British team at the Olympics, at Tokyo in 1964.

DONCASTER, THE RACECOURSE c1955 D41009

QUIZ QUESTIONS

Answers on page 52.

1. Which of the famous literary Brontë sisters is associated with Scarborough?

2. Which famous artist was commissioned to paint Huddersfield in 1965?

3. Since medieval times, the title of Duke of York has traditionally been given to the second son of the sovereign. How many Dukes of York have eventually been crowned king?

4. What was meant by the term 'rattening', which was used in Sheffield in the 19th century?

5. Which visitor to Leeds received a tankard filled with gold in 1646?

6. Which famous chain of High Street shops started on a market stall in Leeds in 1884?

7. The Cartwright Memorial Hall in Bradford was designed to hold the city's art treasures, but who is it named after, and what was his contribution to Bradford?

8. Titus Salt's model village of Saltaire, built in the mid 19th century, was missing two facilities usually found in towns at that time – what were they?

9. Which famous name in aviation history was born in Hull in 1903?

10. How did events in Whitby in ancient times give us the expression 'a moveable feast'?

LEEDS, THE POST OFFICE AND REVENUE OFFICE 1897 39088

SELBY, THE CROSS AND GOWTHORPE 1903 49865

RECIPE

YORKSHIRE CURD TART

The distinguishing and traditional characteristic of Yorkshire Curd Tart is allspice (or 'clove pepper' as it was also known) but this may not be to modern tastes, so mixed spice can be substituted for the ground allspice if preferred.

<u>For the pastry:</u>
115g/4oz butter, diced
225g/8oz plain flour
1 egg yolk

<u>For the filling:</u>
A large pinch of ground allspice, or mixed
  spice if preferred
90g/3½ oz sugar
3 eggs, beaten
Grated rind and juice of 1 lemon
40g/1½ oz melted butter
450g/1 lb curd cheese, or cottage cheese if
  curd cheese is hard to find
75g/3oz raisins or sultanas

To make the pastry: rub the butter into the flour until the mixture resembles fine breadcrumbs. Stir the egg yolk into the flour mixture with a little water to bind the dough together. Turn the dough on to a lightly floured surface, knead lightly and form into a ball. Roll out the pastry thinly and use to line a 20cm (8 inch) fluted loose-bottomed flan tin. Chill for 15 minutes.

To make the filling: mix the ground allspice or mixed spice with the sugar, then stir in the eggs, lemon rind and juice, melted butter, curd or cottage cheese and dried fruit. Pour the filling into the chilled pastry case, then bake in a pre-heated oven (190°C/375°F/Gas Mark 5) for about 40 minutes until the pastry is cooked and the filling is lightly set and golden brown. Serve still slightly warm, cut into wedges with cream.

RECIPE

YORKSHIRE PARKIN

The black treacle gives this the true dark parkin colour.

300ml/ ½ pint milk
225g/8oz golden syrup
225g/8oz black treacle
115g/4oz butter or margarine
50g/2oz dark brown sugar
450g/1 lb plain flour
Half a teaspoonful of bicarbonate of soda
1½ teaspoonfuls of ground ginger
350g/12oz medium oatmeal
1 egg, beaten

Pre-heat the oven to 180°C/350°F/Gas Mark 4.

Put the milk, syrup, treacle, butter or margarine and sugar into a saucepan and heat gently, stirring all the time, until the mixture has melted and is smooth. Take care not to let the mixture boil. When it has mixed together, take it off the heat and leave to cool for a few minutes. Put the flour, bicarbonate of soda, ginger and oatmeal into a large bowl and mix together. Make a well in the centre, pour in the beaten egg, then gradually pour in the milk and syrup mixture, stirring all the time, until it has formed a smooth batter.

Grease a 20cm (8 inch) square cake tin, and line the bottom with greaseproof paper. Pour the batter into the tin. Bake in the pre-heated oven for about 45 minutes, until the surface of the parkin is firm to the touch. Allow the parkin to cool in the tin for a few minutes, then turn out on to a wire rack to cool completely. Cut into pieces when cool, and store in an airtight tin, preferably for 3 days, before eating.

QUIZ ANSWERS

1. Anne Brontë, the youngest of the famous Brontë sisters, loved Scarborough and visited many times; she used the town as the background to her novel 'Agnes Grey'. She died in Scarborough in 1849, and was buried in the churchyard of St Mary's Church in the town.

2. L S Lowrie. It can be seen in Huddersfield Art Gallery.

3. Six Dukes of York have become reigning monarchs. They are: Edward IV, Henry VIII, Charles I, James II, George V and George VI.

4. 'Rattening', which originally referred to rats destroying human belongings, took on a more sinister meaning during the 'Sheffield Outrages' of the second half of the 19th century, when trade unionists were accused of threatening non-union members by means of arson, intimidation and murder. It became the term used for the confiscation of a workman's tolls on behalf of trade societies to persuade workers to join a union or to make them stop working for masters paying less than the recommended rate.

5. In 1646, during the Civil War, Charles I was held prisoner for one night at the Red Hall in Upper Head Row. One of the stories surrounding the king's short stay in Leeds concerns John Harrison, a wealthy landowner. Harrison asked permission to meet the king and present him with a tankard of ale. The king accepted Harrison's offer, and on opening the lid of the tankard he found it full of golden guineas, which 'his Majesty did, with much celerity, hasten to secrete about his royal person'.

6. Marks & Spencer. The Lithuanian immigrant Michael Marks opened his first Penny Bazaar stall in Leeds in 1884, selling buttons, wool, socks and stockings, before moving to Skipton where he co-founded Marks and Spencer with Tom Spencer.

7. It was named in memory of Dr Edmund Cartwright, who invented the power loom that brought so much wealth to Bradford.

8. Only two things were missing from Titus Salt's model village of Saltaire – a pub (he was firmly against alcohol) and a pawnshop.

9. Hull was the birthplace of the aviation pioneer Amy Johnson (1903-1941), hailed as a national heroine when she became the first female pilot to fly solo from Britain to Australia, at the age of 26, in 1930. She began the historic flight in her de Havilland DH60 Gipsy Moth G-AAAH from Croydon Airfield on 5 May 1930, and landed at Port Darwin, on the northern tip of Australia, nineteen days later, after flying 9,960 miles on a dangerous and eventful trip. She is commemorated in Hull by a statue in Prospect Street.

10. In AD664 the Synod of Whitby was held at Whitby Abbey to resolve the differences between Celtic and Roman Christianity, particularly over calculating the date of Easter. Following the synod, the English Church was unified under the Roman discipline, and the date of Easter Day was settled as the first Sunday after the Paschal full moon. Because Easter itself is a holy day whose date is not fixed to a particular day of the calendar year, the dates of all the other Christian festivals – or 'feasts' – which are linked to it are also changeable, in response to the date of Easter for that year, and thus are known as 'moveable feasts'. Easter itself can also be called a 'moveable feast'.

FRANCIS FRITH

PIONEER VICTORIAN PHOTOGRAPHER

Francis Frith, founder of the world-famous photographic archive, was a complex and multi-talented man. A devout Quaker and a highly successful Victorian businessman, he was philosophical by nature and pioneering in outlook. By 1855 he had already established a wholesale grocery business in Liverpool, and sold it for the astonishing sum of £200,000, which is the equivalent today of over £15,000,000. Now in his thirties, and captivated by the new science of photography, Frith set out on a series of pioneering journeys up the Nile and to the Near East.

INTRIGUE AND EXPLORATION

He was the first photographer to venture beyond the sixth cataract of the Nile. Africa was still the mysterious 'Dark Continent', and Stanley and Livingstone's historic meeting was a decade into the future. The conditions for picture taking confound belief. He laboured for hours in his wicker dark-room in the sweltering heat of the desert, while the volatile chemicals fizzed dangerously in their trays. Back in London he exhibited his photographs and was 'rapturously cheered' by members of the Royal Society. His reputation as a photographer was made overnight.

VENTURE OF A LIFE-TIME

By the 1870s the railways had threaded their way across the country, and Bank Holidays and half-day Saturdays had been made obligatory by Act of Parliament. All of a sudden the working man and his family were able to enjoy days out, take holidays, and see a little more of the world.

With typical business acumen, Francis Frith foresaw that these new tourists would enjoy having souvenirs to commemorate their days out. For the next thirty years he travelled the country by train and by pony and trap, producing fine photographs of seaside resorts and beauty spots that were keenly bought by millions of Victorians. These prints were painstakingly pasted into family albums and pored over during the dark nights of winter, rekindling precious memories of summer excursions. Frith's studio was soon supplying retail shops all over the country, and by 1890 F Frith & Co had become the greatest specialist photographic publishing company in the world, with over 2,000 sales outlets, and pioneered the picture postcard.

FRANCIS FRITH'S LEGACY

Francis Frith had died in 1898 at his villa in Cannes, his great project still growing. By 1970 the archive he created contained over a third of a million pictures showing 7,000 British towns and villages.

Frith's legacy to us today is of immense significance and value, for the magnificent archive of evocative photographs he created provides a unique record of change in the cities, towns and villages throughout Britain over a century and more. Frith and his fellow studio photographers revisited locations many times down the years to update their views, compiling for us an enthralling and colourful pageant of British life and character.

We are fortunate that Frith was dedicated to recording the minutiae of everyday life. For it is this sheer wealth of visual data, the painstaking chronicle of changes in dress, transport, street layouts, buildings, housing and landscape that captivates us so much today, offering us a powerful link with the past and with the lives of our ancestors.

Computers have now made it possible for Frith's many thousands of images to be accessed almost instantly. The archive offers every one of us an opportunity to examine the places where we and our families have lived and worked down the years. Its images, depicting our shared past, are now bringing pleasure and enlightenment to millions around the world a century and more after his death.

For further information visit: www.francisfrith.com

INTERIOR DECORATION

Frith's photographs can be seen framed and as giant wall murals in thousands of pubs, restaurants, hotels, banks, retail stores and other public buildings throughout Britain. These provide interesting and attractive décor, generating strong local interest and acting as a powerful reminder of gentler days in our increasingly busy and frenetic world.

FRITH PRODUCTS

All Frith photographs are available as prints and posters in a variety of different sizes and styles. In the UK we also offer a range of other gift and stationery products illustrated with Frith photographs, although many of these are not available for delivery outside the UK – see our web site for more information on the products available for delivery in your country.

THE INTERNET

Over 100,000 photographs of Britain can be viewed and purchased on the Frith web site. The web site also includes memories and reminiscences contributed by our customers, who have personal knowledge of localities and of the people and properties depicted in Frith photographs. If you wish to learn more about a specific town or village you may find these reminiscences fascinating to browse. Why not add your own comments if you think they would be of interest to others? See **www.francisfrith.com**

PLEASE HELP US BRING FRITH'S PHOTOGRAPHS TO LIFE

Our authors do their best to recount the history of the places they write about. They give insights into how particular towns and villages developed, they describe the architecture of streets and buildings, and they discuss the lives of famous people who lived there. But however knowledgeable our authors are, the story they tell is necessarily incomplete.